TRAINER'S GUIDE

Creativity and Problem Solving

Phil Lowe

A Complete Package For A One-Day Training Workshop

KOGAN PAGE

PUBLISHED IN ASSOCIATION WITH
HARBRIDGE CONSULTING
GROUP LIMITED

Publisher's Note

Every possible effort has been made to ensure that the information contained in this book is accurate at the time of going to press, and the publishers and authors cannot accept responsibility for any errors or omissions, however caused. No responsibility for loss or damage occasioned to any person acting, or refraining from action, as a result of the material in this publication can be accepted by the editor, the publisher or any of the authors.

South Asian Edition 2007
Reprinted 2008, 2010

Kogan Page India Private Limited
4737/23 Ansari Road,
Daryaganj
New Delhi 110 002

This edition is for sale in the Indian subcontinent only. Not for export elsewhere.

ISBN: 978-81-7554-364-5

Published by Vinod Vasishtha for Kogan Page India Private Limited,
4737/23 Ansari Road, Daryaganj, New Delhi - 110 002.

Printed and bound at Raj Press, R-3, Inderpuri, New Delhi - 110 012.

The Kogan Page One Day Workshop Package Series

Series Editor's preface

This series of workshops is for organizations that wish to undertake high-quality management training, but lack either the time or the resources to develop their own in-house programmes. Each workshop is accompanied by full notes, which means that it can be taught with confidence by someone who has familiarity with, but does not have expert status in, the subject.

All workshops have been designed with the needs of busy managers in mind, and have been prepared by people who have extensive experience in the design, development and teaching of in-company training courses, as well as considerable understanding of the pressures on organizations and individuals.

Each workshop takes one working day, and strikes a balance between exercises to be undertaken by participants and essential inputs from the person running the course. Masters have been provided from which overhead projector slides can be made, giving good visual aids to support all lectures. The trainer can of course modify these sessions if required to suit personal style (perhaps adding some examples from the organization itself). The masters could, for example, be put on to flip charts if this method of presentation is preferred.

Although workshops are intended to stand alone, they can be linked into longer courses. Because the programmes deal with fundamental management skills, they can be used at a variety of levels within an organization, the limitation being the knowledge and skill level of the managers.

There are two ways of arranging the workshops. The first, and probably the most traditional, is to organize by peer groups, so that levels of experience are roughly matched. This is partly because the more experienced upper-middle managers will have different issues to discuss than will, say, new graduate management recruits or supervisors, and learning may be enhanced if the discussions take place among people who share an understanding of these issues. The prime purpose of this approach would be to enhance personal skills.

An alternative approach might be to organize attendance on a divisional or section basis, so that several levels from the same organizational unit attend. Here, in addition to the increase in personal skills, the aim would be to improve the way in which the whole unit manages. Although potentially beneficial, particularly with topics such as communication, this approach carries a higher risk and should only be attempted when there is strong backing from the head of the unit and his or her most senior managers.

A key aim of the series is to make it easier for organizations to run workshops which are held completely in-house, and to make it economic for these to be run for a relatively small number of participants. For many small- to medium-sized companies, particularly those in which management training is a part-time or nonexistent function, in-house training has traditionally been an uneconomic option, which has either meant sending managers on external public courses, or has made it difficult for any training to be undertaken at all. The benefits of an internal workshop include:

- A common understanding can be built up throughout the organization.
- Issues which are germane to the organization can be raised and discussed.
- A confidential environment makes it easier to share real problems.
- Such training can be part of a mechanism to build a common culture for the organization.
- The organization has full flexibility in when and where it runs workshops, how frequently, and who should attend.

The workshops can be run for between six and 20 participants. Although it may be possible to drop below the minimum, this would make it more difficult to get full value from the exercises. Above 20 it becomes hard to ensure participation. An optimum number would be 12–15 people on each session, because this gives scope for different views to be aired in a participative way. Most organizations have a room available which will hold this number of people without becoming overcrowded or unfriendly.

A wide range of workshops is being developed to cover the main management and interpersonal skills that are needed for managers to operate effectively at all levels of the organization. These will build into a library of courses, enabling the organization to select those titles which fit its priority needs.

In designing the series we have drawn on over 40 years of experience which my organization has in consultancy, management development and management training, supported by original research into best practice and new management concepts. We hope that the results will help your organization to improve performance through improved management.

D E Hussey
Managing Director
Harbridge Consulting Group Ltd

A note on the materials

This teaching pack contains all the materials required for the one-day programme, arranged as follows:

- A trainer's binder containing guidelines for preparation, trainer's notes for the programme, and masters from which to copy handouts and acetates for overhead projection.

- A binder containing all participants' material.

The material has been arranged in this way to give trainers the freedom either to interleave the pages, so that notes for the participants appear alongside their relevant teaching notes, or to keep the participants' material as a separate reference document.

The Trainer's Notes section effectively forms a rough 'script' of the course. Cues for showing overhead slides are given in italics at the appropriate point.

The binder is single-sided throughout, to give trainers room to write any notes, and to help them to collate the material in whichever way suits them best.

Contents

Timetable

9.00	Introduction
9.30	Problem identification and definition
10.30	Coffee
10.45	Case study presentations
11.15	Generating creative solutions
12.15	Choosing the best solution
1.00	Lunch
2.00	Choosing the best solution – continued
3.15	Planning for implementation
3.45	Tea
4.15	Action planning
5.30	Close workshop

Materials required

Furniture

Main room

Tables and chairs for all participants and trainer
Flipchart and thick flipchart pens
Projection screen
Table big enough for the overhead projector and the overhead slides (next to it)
Table for the course materials
Table (or lectern) for the tutor's notes

Syndicate rooms (if used)

Tables and chairs for participants
Spare chair for when trainer 'sits in'
Flipchart and thick flipchart pens
Dictionaries (for creativity exercise)

Stationery

Set of course materials } for each participant
Folder, binders etc. for handouts } for each participant
A4 writing pads and pens
Stapler
Hole punch
Pencil sharpener
Spare pens and pencils
Spare blank overhead slides and overhead pens
Blu-tack or masking tape (for hanging flipchart paper on walls if needed)

Accommodation and room layout

The main training room must be large enough to accommodate the participants and equipment without them being squashed together.

The programme includes discussion exercises for pairs or groups of three, and if people are too close to the neighbouring group they frequently feel inhibited and therefore get less out of the exercise.

The layout of the room may place participants round a 'u' shape of tables or in small groups of, say, four, around separate tables, 'cabaret' style. Leave enough space at tne front for you and the equipment.

Set the room up the day before if possible, or at least well in advance of the participants' arrival, so that you can move any furniture as necessary and be satisfied and comfortable with the layout. There is nothing worse than heaving furniture around while newly arrived participants, possibly mildly apprehensive, are milling aimlessly about.

Put the flipchart on whichever side works better for you: are you left- or right-handed, for instance?

Avoid sitting behind a table, 'schoolteacher' fashion. It can be helpful to have notes on a table beside you, rather than in front.

For the practical exercises, try and arrange for separate small rooms to be available. People will concentrate better away from other groups. Avoid 'eyeball-to-eyeball' across-a-table layout for these syndicate rooms.

Session timings

The workshop timing, and particularly that of the exercises, will be significantly affected by participants' prior experience. You should use your knowledge of the group, and the extent to which internal organizational issues need to be addressed by the workshop, in reviewing the schedule and deciding on the start time.

Some general points to remember:

- If you are behind schedule, do not let it develop into a habit. There is a lot to get through.
- You may be able to 'claw back' time by making the lunch break shorter, if necessary.
- If you are ahead of schedule, consider whether you are encouraging participants to be thorough in discussing and trying out what has been covered so far.
- When people are nervous they are more likely to be superficial and speedy; as they warm up they are likely to use all the time allocated.

Pre-workshop preparation

Some time prior to the workshop, participants should be contacted and asked to perform one small preparation task.

In order to gain maximum benefit from the day, each participant will be given the opportuntity to work on a real-life problem from their own day-to-day work. Accordingly, by the day of the workshop each participant should have prepared a short summary of:

- The particular work-related problem they face
- What makes it a problem (i.e. what is hindering a solution)
- Why it is their problem (as opposed to anyone else's).

Examples of problems might be: having to implement new working practices within a department; having a workload bigger than the individual can cope with; trying to finalize a departmental budget; having to identify particular customer requirements. There are no criteria for what makes a suitable problem; anything is fair game.

Participants will not need to share their summaries during the day; they are for their own reference, although the trainer might find it useful to receive copies in advance of the workshop.

1. Introduction

Timing guidelines

		Minutes (approx)
9.00	Warm up: 'Top of the head'	10
	Warm up: nine dots	5
	Problem-solving model	15
		——
9.30		30

Introduction

- Welcome participants to what will be an active day.
- Introduce yourself, if necessary: who you are, your job and responsibilities.
- The day will be a mixture of input from the tutor, outlining ideas and approaches, and of exercises, analysis and discussion by the participants. Talk through the timetable and where the practical work fits in.

Slide 1 'We will be looking in our work today at a structured approach to problem solving. At the end of the day you will be able to:

- Define accurately the nature and extent of a problem
- Use creativity techniques to generate potential solutions
- Decide on and apply the most appropriate criteria to select the best solution
- Apply these skills to a real-life work issue.'

Warm-up: 'Top of the head'

- Acknowledge the point that a large part of the day's work is concerned with the subject of creativity, and that many people find it a daunting subject. The standard response of people faced with a creative task is: 'I can't think of anything new: there's nothing in my head.' This is a quick exercise designed to show that everyone always has something in their head.

- Ask participants to turn to page 5 of their binders. They can use the blank page provided for this exercise.

- Everyone in the room – you and the participants – is going to count out loud from 1 to 100. At the same time, participants are to write on the blank page. They can write whatever they like. They are not to worry about whether it makes sense. If they are doing the exercise properly they will not be able to think about what they are writing. They are to start writing at the moment everyone starts counting and finish at the point when everyone reaches 100. There are two rules:

  - They musn't stop counting

  - They musn't stop writing.

- You will need to be extra vigilant and force people to count out loud, also to keep writing. Several participants will probably feel obliged to write something coherent: in order to do this they will either have to stop counting, or to stop writing to think of what to write next.

- When this exercise works, the writer will produce a pure 'stream of consciousness' that is almost dreamlike. At the worst, someone will have written 'one, two three, four, five' ... etc. Encourage a few volunteers to read theirs out – most examples will cause some amusement.

- The only point to make is that all of us – all the time – carry something loosely creative in our heads. What we have to do is harness it.

Warm up: nine dots

Slide 2 Put up the slide showing the nine dots. Refer participants to page 6 of their binders and tell them this is a brain teaser, with many possible solutions. They have to find a way of covering all nine dots with no more than four straight lines, which must be connected to each other (i.e. no lifting the pen from the paper).

- This is not an original puzzle: some participants may have seen it before. Encourage those who have the 'right' answer not to share it. At this stage of the workshop treat it as very much a throwaway exercise: there is a point but that will not emerge until later in the day.

- Do stress, however, that this is not a test of how creative a person you are (puzzles like this are often presented as such). The premise of this workshop is that everyone can be creative: this requires one particular type of creativity.

A problem-solving model

Slide 3 Use this slide to talk through the model which forms the framework of the day's activities. It also appears on page 7 of the participant binders.

- The first step in solving a problem is to identify and define the exact nature of the problem. This may sound obvious, but very often it is not until a problem is broken down into its constituent elements that the 'real' problem becomes apparent.
- Step two is to generate creative solutions. The emphasis here is on possibilities, not what will or will not work in practice.
- Once potential solutions have been generated, they must be evaluated and the most suitable and appropriate solution selected.
- The chosen solution must then be implemented. The considerations of this stage vary considerably with each problem, and so we will not be spending a great deal of time on implementation itself, although there will be a long session in the afternoon in which participants can work on the live problems they have brought with them.

2. Problem identification and definition

Timing guidelines

		Minutes (approx)
9.30	Lecture/discussion	15
	Exercise: Grinding Solutions plc (1)	45
	Coffee break	15
	Presentations	30
		—
11.15		105

Problem identification and definition

Introduction

- The first stage in the effective management of tasks is problem identification and definition. Before a manager can 'do' anything he or she must first consider what it is that needs to be done.

- Problem identification and definition can be divided into three steps:

  1) Identify the apparent problem
  2) Seek and analyse the cause
  3) Define the real problem

Identify the apparent problem

- Very often there is no clearly defined problem to which the manager can come up with solutions. Most problems are messy, ill-defined and hard to spot with no one willing to take responsibility for them. The task of identification and definition is a key skill for any manager but one that is often seen as an impediment to the real business of solutions - taking action and doing things, instead of thinking. There are of course problems that do present themselves as clear cut - but often this means that the implications beyond the immediate situation have not been thought through. Identifying and defining problems uses two key skills: creativity and critical thinking. These two skills are used to transform a messy, ambiguous, vague problem into a more clear-cut analytical framework.

Values and context

- Two areas which cause problems to be fuzzy we can summarize as 'values' and 'context'. 'Values' means all the biases, viewpoints and frames of reference that we, as individuals, bring to a particular issue. It is fairly obvious to any good manager that different individuals will tend to look upon a whole range of problems from a consistent standpoint which, for ease, can be labelled their values. Some people will have values which in management terms orient them towards the task, others towards people. It would also be surprising if the roles and functions of people did not have a large influence – sales being biased towards expansion and growth regardless of the issue, for example. In more general terms, a number of psychological tests will pick up and help individuals understand their own biases.

- 'Context' means the whole range of background variables which again influence the problem although they may only do this very indirectly. Here are all the many assumptions and company parameters. For example, a key contextual factor which most managers would take into account, even if not clarified, would be the overall company purpose and objectives. Linking into this would be the type of people in the organization, the role of the department, and the environment both internally and externally.

- Of course, it would be extremely timewasting to re-examine all these deep contextual issues every time a decision is needed on whether to have a cup of tea or coffee, so usually the context is taken for granted in the form of assumptions. However, the more senior the managers are, the more important the context becomes. Directors, for example, need to be far more aware of the role of their company in relation to society's issues and concerns than, say, a production manager. Sometimes in problem identification there is a need to re-examine basic issues (growth, company purpose, etc.) and this possibility should be allowed for.

Seek and analyse the cause

- Critical thinking is used to judge what the key decisive factors are that affect a problem and to see whether it needs to be redefined. Data and facts need to be collected, if not done so already, to help in this clarification. There are several techniques that are used at this stage to help organize data and ideas so that critical judgements can be made more easily. The techniques are used to organize data visually to help assimilation and any visual presentations such as pie charts, histograms, graphs or flow charts should be used wherever possible. Two of the key techniques are:

    - Fishbone diagrams (Ishikawa)
    - Forcefield analysis

Fishbone diagram (cause and effect)

- After collection of factors and data, three or four key areas into which they can be placed are identified. These will vary but often key groupings used are:

- People
- Processes
- Materials
- Money

Slide 4 shows a sample fishbone diagram from an imaginary company in which the problem is a lack of collaboration between branches. It is simplified as obviously each bone can have several more growing from it.

Force field analysis

- Force field analysis is used to describe a situation in terms of a balance between two sets of forces - helping and hindering. For example: helping forces for low morale could be pay and conditions, hindering forces could be poor supervision, etc.

Slide 5 shows the same imaginary company problem in force field analysis format. Use it to talk participants through the steps.

First, the forces on both sides must be identified. Then they must be weighted in terms of the amount of force they exert. You can bring about change in two ways: by increasing the forces helping change or by reducing the forces resisting change. The most effective way is to weaken the resisting forces. The procedure is as follows:

1. Choose a particular problem that you feel is worthwhile working on.

2. Define in terms of (a) the present situation and (b) the situation you would like to see when it is solved.

3. Make a list of forces impacting on the situation. These can be people, money, time, external factors – anything that could hinder or help you to make a change. When identifying forces, it is helpful to be specific and to draw a force field diagram.

4. On a force field diagram draw the forces with the arrow signifying its strength of each (the longer, the stronger).

5. For each hindering force list the actions you could take that could possibly reduce or eliminate the force.

6. For each helping force, list the actions you could take that could possibly increase the force.

7. Determine the most promising steps you could take towards solving the problem and identify the resources available to help you.

Affinity diagram

- An affinity diagram can be used to uncover the various aspects of a particular issue. It is particularly useful when issues are large and complex or when a significant breakthrough is needed. Examples might include the need to identify expectations of specific customers and customer segments, or to isolate the issues involved in implementing a new IT system.

Slide 6

1. Generate – using brainstorming techniques – a full list of all the issues involved in the situation selected (e.g. all issues relating to closer collaboration between a company's sales branches).

2. Write each issue on a card, Post-It or even magnetic hexagon. Each issue should have a noun and a verb (e.g. 'documentation gets lost').

3. Place all cards, Post-Its, etc. on a flat surface so each member of the group can see easily.

4. Move the cards around until there is agreement about the clusters. Each cluster forms a grouping with similarity of meaning.

Slide 7

5. Label the clusters by giving each a 'header' note that captures the central theme in no more than five words (e.g. 'lost documentation').

6. Consolidate the result onto a flipchart or large sheet of paper so the overall problem can be seen.

Problem definition

- Clear problem definitions are brief and to the point. They are specific and concrete. They say what the problem is without implying a particular solution in the definition. They are also understandable to all those involved.

- Linked to the one-line problem definition should be a list of criteria which give guidelines and parameters defining acceptable ranges of solutions. These will emerge from the analysis. For example:

Problem Definition Fall in sales in last period

Criteria	*Must:*	Sales up to budget targets by next period
	Would be nice:	Recover lost sales from this period

- Finally, the whole question of problem ownership emerges. There needs to be a clear definition of the boundaries of ownership. It is all too easy to get drawn into solving other people's problems and neglecting the ones which are your own. This is where the area of prioritizing and delegation comes in. Once the problem is identified and defined - who owns it and needs to take responsibility for it?

Exercise: Grinding Solutions plc (1)

- Refer participants to the brief on pages 15 – 22 of their binders.

- Emphasize that at this stage, no solutions or options for tackling the problem are required. The time is to be used to work at identifying as specifically as possible the problem and its constituent elements.

- Suggested timing is 15 minutes to read the case, 30 minutes to tackle the exercise.

- Divide participants into groups of up to six. Ideally there should be no more than three for the sake of timing the presentations. If three groups emerge, it may be worth assigning one technique to each group (i.e. one group uses forcefield analysis, one uses a fishbone and one an affinity diagram).

- At the end of the exercise, break for coffee before the groups present back.

Presentations

- Don't let groups off the hook: it is all very well deciding that the problem is that the PT 121 Grinder-Sorter isn't selling as well as expcted, but being precise about all the individual elements and factors is what will ultimately yield a viable solution.

- Make it clear that the case is based on a real-life company. What that company did will be revealed later in the day (after the second part of this exercise), but the fishbone diagram on the slide will serve for now to tie up the discussion.

3. Generating creative solutions

Timing guidelines

		Minutes (approx)
11.15	Lecture/discussion	15
	Exercise: Morphological analysis	30
	Presentations	15
		—
12.15		60

Introduction

- Before the session, have a flipchart prepared with a rough drawing like the one below.

- Say to participants that before starting the next session, you'd like everyone to give you some comments on 'this' and unveil the illustration.

- Go round the room getting comments from each participant in turn. Most if not all participants will make a negative comment ('The wheel's in the wrong place', 'It's not drawn very well', 'The handle's too short' and so on). If this happens, respond visibly by becoming less and less enthusiastic and give up half-way round the room. If anyone gives you a positive comment, thank them enthusiastically and genuinely.

- When you have had enough, ask the simple question 'What are you doing to my idea?' The answer you want, which someone should come up with, is 'killing it'.

- Make the point that most of us (yourself included!) will tend to criticize a new idea before complimenting it: it seems to be an instinctive human reaction, at least in the UK. And it is for this reason that most of us hesitate before suggesting a new idea or a creative solution to a problem – we are afraid of having our idea ridiculed or destroyed.

- Ask how your diagram, with some improvements, might be a very good design for a wheelbarrow. Engineers or physicists may be able to suggest a reason (it pivots in the middle because of not having a wheel at the front, therefore requiring less energy to lift the load). It may not be perfect – but there would have been no harm in saying: 'That's a very interesting design for a wheelbarrow – perhaps if you made the handle a bit longer it would make better use of the pivot...' and so on.

Slide 8 This quotation from Edward de Bono's book *Lateral Thinking for Managers* (see reading list) ties up the point.

Slide 9 Now is the moment to unveil the solution to the nine dots puzzle. If you prefer, you could draw the nine dots on a flipchart (before the session) and invite anyone who thinks they have a solution to come and draw it on. In any case, the slide gives the 'model answer'. Don't forget that, in order to keep in the split of this particular session (especially in the light of the de Bono quotation) anyone who has any solution which meets the criteria can be deemed to have succeeded.

- The point to be made is that the problem in this case cannot be solved without taking a step back and looking afresh at the situation – to avoid being constrained by the imaginary box created by the dots.

- Edward de Bono coined the phrase 'lateral thinking' to describe this process of breaking away from our normal approaches to problems in order to generate as many potential solutions as possible. De Bono talks about 'tethering factors': these are the restrictions on creativity which tend to strangle new ideas at birth.

  For example, at a very basic level, someone given the task of ordering new furniture for the office will instinctively reach for the catalogue left by the office supplies rep last time he or she called. Why? Because that is the way office furniture has always been ordered. Getting away from this tethering factor could be something as simple as ringing every supplier in the phone book to generate as many ideas as possible; or perhaps talking to people in the office about what kind of furniture they would like in an ideal world. Why be restricted to office furniture? Why not have armchairs if that makes people more comfortable and happier in their work surroundings? (There may be plenty of good reasons why not, of course: but the assumption that there will is in itself a tethering factor, because it stops the idea from even being suggested.)

- In the case of the 'nine dots' exercise, the tethering factor which prevents many people from solving the puzzle is the way that our brains perceive the dots as forming a box: we assume that we are not 'allowed' to go outside this box, but without doing so we cannot solve the problem. We tend also to assume that we have to use a normal size pen or pencil to draw the lines: why not use a paintbrush thick enough to cover all the dots with one straight line? This is what de Bono meant by lateral thinking: a sideways step away from our inherited assumptions about the 'right way' to do things in order to generate more potential options.

Brainstorming

- Brainstorming sessions are the traditional forum for generating new ideas. Many people are frightened of brainstorming sessions, either because they are worried about having to come up with a brilliant idea, or because we think of them as undisciplined and therefore difficult to control. If these worries are inhibiting creative thinking, then the solution is to impose some rules on the session: far from restricting creativity, the right kind of rules can make a session far more productive, since everyone knows what is going on and how the meeting is going to work.

Slide 10 There are some basic rules which we can impose on a brainstorming session:

- *Limit the length of the session.* Don't go on and on if people's ideas are drying up. Decide in advance how long you are going to spend (preferably a short, focused session: half to one hour) and if ideas are still flowing at the end, arrange another session rather than over-egging .

- *Don't interrupt.* Allow other people the space they need to get their ideas out. You may think yours is better – but you'll get your turn too!

- *Don't evaluate.* That would reinforce the idea that there is already a right and wrong solution. Evaluation can be done when all the potential solutions have been generated. If it is done too early it is being done on the basis of 'vertical' thinking (e.g. what we did last time).

- *Elect a chairperson and a scribe.* You need someone to keep the meeting on track and moving along. The chairperson ensures the rules are followed. It is also essential to have someone to capture every idea on paper, in order that each can be properly evaluated at a later time. The briefest, quickest idea may well be the best – but may well get forgotten if no proper record is kept.

- *Have a structure.* Don't let the meeting sprawl. Be clear about what the problem is that you are tackling, any parameters on its solution, and any essential items that the meeting has to tackle. Then agree an agenda accordingly.

- *Use tools.* Good ideas don't arise magically from the ether – at least not for most people. If you find it difficult to come up with creative ideas to order, there are techniques you can use to aid the lateral thinking process. Two of them are listed on the slide.

Random word generating

- This is a straightforward technique for getting individuals or teams out of an ideas 'log jam', and away from tethering factors. The technique involves opening a dictionary or any book at random and choosing a word, without thinking about either the word's meaning or the problem being tackled. The word chosen must then be linked to the problem using as many meanings, nuances and connections as possible.

- The participants' binder works through an example of random word generating (pages 27 – 28). The trainer may wish to supply his or her own example more pertinent to the organization. (Just to reassure you, the example in the binder was produced 'cold' by the author, and it may be worth producing your own example, resisting the temptation to cheat: the rough edges give it veracity.)

Morphological analysis

- Morphological analysis takes the random word generation process a stage further, by combining nouns with random adjectives to create new possibilities for existing ideas. Summarized below are the steps explored in the participants' binder. As with random word generating, the example in the binder was produced unprepared using a dictionary. The trainer may wish to substitute his or her own example, or get participants to supply appropriate words.

  – *Step one*: Assemble a list of four or more nouns which are relevant to the problem in hand.

- *Step two:* Using random word generating, *but limiting yourself to adjectives*, generate four or more 'qualities' which things can have. Make them completely random – don't attempt to link them yet to the list of nouns.

Slide 11 *Step three:* Build a matrix with the nouns along the top and the adjectives down the side.

Step four: At each intersection, brainstorm the possibilities suggested by the combination of adjective and noun. Talk participants through this if you are using your own example – get them to join in the process of developing the possibilities suggested at each intersection.

Exercise: morphological analysis

- Morpholigical analysis is not appropriate for every problem, but participants are unlikely to find any true potential benefit in the technique unless they are given an opportuntity to work it through for themselves.
- Divide participants into groups of around six members each. The brief is on page 32 of their binders.
- The groups will need to be policed diligently to make sure they are keeping clear of any tethering factors, and are following the brainstorming guidelines.
- Give groups the opportunity to make a brief presentation of their ideas, to ensure everyone understands the essence of them (and hopefully to ensure everyone is entertained by what should be a lively and creative selection).

4. Choosing the best solution

Timing guidelines

		Minutes (approx)
12.15	Lecture/discussion	15
	Exercise: Evaluating and selecting options	30
	Lunch break	60
	Exercise presentations	15
	Exercise: Grinding Solutions plc (2)	30
	Presentations	30
		—
3.15		180

Break for lunch until 2.00

Introduction

- The reason for excluding evaluation from the process of generating potential solutions is that if ideas are evaluated too early in the process, there is a double risk that the idea may not have had a fair hearing, and that the evaluation is too subjective. The process of evaluating and selecting the successful solution must wait until all the potential solutions are fully developed.

Slide 12 The slide emphasizes this point. By separating the evaluation from the generation of ideas, we can evaluate a potential solution in terms of the context of the problem: in terms of this workshop, that will tend to mean the organizational or departmental context. The question to ask when selecting an option is not, 'What do I think?' but, 'What is important to the organization/the people I work with/those who will be affected by this option?'

As with the generation of potential solutions, there are a number of tools and techniques which can be used to make this process less subjective and more systematic.

Slide 13 The options/criteria matrix is virtually self-explanatory. The options under consideration are itemized along the top, while down the side are listed the essential or desirable criteria which the solution must satisfy. By allocating points to each option against each criterion, ideas can be compared in terms of their total score. If the criteria are mutually agreed, egos should not be too bruised when a personal favourite gets rejected.

Slide 14 The risk/payoff matrix is beautifully simple. Talk participants through it and get them to suggest at each point the likely action:

- *High Risk/High Payoff:* If the payoff is potentially high, this option should be pursued – but you should cover yourself against the risk.

- *High Risk/Low Payoff:* This should be avoided at all costs.

- *Low Risk/Low Payoff:* This is worth doing if there's nothing better available, but a higher return should be sought from the successful option.

- *Low Risk/High Payoff:* What are you waiting for?!

Slide 15 Most management decisions can be seen as a function of quality x acceptance. The former is about how technically right the decision needs to be, the latter about how willing people need to be to go along with the option. Certain problems will 'belong' in certain boxes:

- *High Quality/High Acceptance:* A move to a new office involves satisfying specific technical requirements, and needs to be accepted by virtually everyone if it is to succeed.

- *High Quality/Low Acceptance:* The purchase of a new computer system will need to meet a high quality threshold, but tends not to need a great deal of consultation with employees in general.

- *Low Quality/High Acceptance:* Issues to do with hours of work (such as when to set a lunch break for example) have little to do with technical exactness but can cause riots among staff if they resent the decision.

- *Low Quality/Low Acceptance:* Changing the colour of the office walls may cause some people to have apoplexy but ultimately neither quality nor acceptance may be an issue.

Exercise: evaluating and selecting options

- Refer participants to the brief on page 37 of their binders.

- They are to remain in the same groups as for the morphological analysis exercise. Each group is given the list of new ideas generated by one of the other groups so that no group is evaluating their own ideas. They are to follow the brief in order to pick one 'winner' from their given list – and to defend their choice by talking the others through their selection process afterwards.

- As with the first options exercise, it would be a good idea to keep a close eye on the syndicate groups to ensure they're following the 'rules'.

- Break for lunch at the end of the exercise. When the groups reconvene after lunch, ask for a very brief piece of feedback from each as to which option they selected and why. What problems, if any, did they face which made the selection process particularly tricky?

Exercise: Grinding Solutions plc (2)

- Participants are to return to the groups they were in for the previous case study exercise.

- This time, they are to take the problem identificaton material they produced and use it as the basis to generate and select options to address the problem the company faces. The brief is on page 38 of their binders.

- When the groups present their plans, question them critically as before. On the following pages is a summary of what the real-life company on which this disguised case study is based, did to solve its problem: use this material as you think fit to provide some form of 'model' answer.

What the real company did

The Board of Grinding Solutions plc identified several critical issues that were affecting the PT 121 Grinder-Sorter. Before focusing in on them specifically, they agreed that there was a need to review their own Board procedures and the way that they worked together, especially in light of their non-communication. They agreed that meetings were not well run and that there seemed to be little clarity of roles and functions. Their planning and monitoring processes left a great deal to be desired as the PT 121 issues should have been dealt with several months before.

The key issues specific to the PT 121 were:

- **Production**

  The assembly process clearly needed streamlining. Production costs, if cut, would allow for more distributor margins or a price cut. The chief product engineer was asked to work with the Production Director to change the line as soon as possible. The Managing Director and the Technical Director agreed that they would accept any conclusions reached.

- **Staff Morale**

  Implementing the above would need the Production staff to be kept fully informed. Consultations with the supervisors and the shop steward would take place with an assurance that no redundancies were contemplated. The staff would be allowed to return to their previous tea break procedure and to be involved in the replanning of the assembly line.

- **Lack of Incentives**

It seemed very clear that both the sales reps and the distributors felt that they were not being rewarded enough for selling the PT 121. This was especially true because of its complexity. Incentives to both should be increased. This should help retain sales reps and distributors.

- **Lack of Training**

All those involved seemed to lack awareness of the complexities and benefits of the PT Grinder-Sorter. By improving technical product training and linking this to sales and promotional literature, a number of key issues could be resolved. More units should be sold and there should be less customer problems and more satisfaction. The premium over the rival products could be more clearly stated. In addition, Mary Brown could be brought into the project team in order to discover what she was doing so well.

The management felt that the steel price rises, bearing costs or quality, gear alloy costs or surplus inventory of parts were not relevant at the moment. The advertising budget was seen as adequate – efforts from the sales team should go into better promotional literature and training. The potential strike might become an issue in the future but it was not felt to be directly relevant to the PT Grinder-Sorter issue at the moment. The team were concerned about the attitude of the field engineering force to the customer and customer relations training for them was seen as a necessity for the future.

5. Planning for implementation

Timing guidelines

		Minutes (approx)
3.15	Exercise: Planners and Operators	30
	Tea break	15
	Debrief	15
		——
4.15		60

Exercise: planners and operators

- This exercise relies on giving as little as possible away to participants. Announce only that they will be undertaking a team problem-solving exercise.

- Divide them into groups of three or four members each. There must be an even number of groups (if there are two or three people left over, they can perform a useful function as observers).

- Each group will be either a planning group or an operating group. There should be an equal number of each. Set the exercise up in the following order:

Handout 1 Give one of the planning groups a copy of Handout 1 (Planners' briefing sheet). Say to them: 'You are planners. Here is your brief. When the exercise begins you are to go to [*whichever syndicate room you allocate*]'.

Handout 2 Give one of the operating groups a copy of Handout 2 (Operators' briefing sheet). Say to them: 'You are operators. Here is your brief. You are attached to the planning group in [*the room you just allocated*] but you will be based in this room'.

- Allocate rooms to the other planning groups, alternating with operating groups so that all operators know which planning group they are attached to. Each planning group should be allocated a different room, but the operators should all be based in the main classroom.

- When everyone knows where are they are to go, announce that the exercise has started and send the planners off.

- During the set-up, or at any other time, answer all questions by saying 'You have been given a brief. I can't answer any questions'.

- If you have designated any observers, allocate one to each planning room and tell them simply to record what the planners do. If you have no observers, try and observe as much as you can yourself.

- The main point of this exercise is to demonstrate how job titles and organizational hierarchies can create powerful tethering factors which hamper the efficient implementation of solutions to problems. This exercise could be over within a few minutes: all the planning group needs to do is call the operators in and show them the planning brief. Both groups can then go out and work together on classifying the doors. What is far more likely to happen is that the planners take their job seriously and use up the 20 minutes devising a complex plan for classifying the doors, which they will have to convey to the operators before the real task can begin.

- The other factor at work is the sketchiness of the brief. Both groups will assume that there is a hidden test at work, and may be unwilling to act on their initiative in case they are not 'supposed to'. The planners are likely to feel they have to compensate for the lack of clear guidance in the brief by creating even more detailed plans; the operators may well interpret their brief as meaning they have to wait until they are called before visiting the planners (in fact the brief tells them to report before the end of the exercise, without specifying when). If any operators decide to visit the planners, they may be told to go away because the planners haven't finished planning. Note down any events like this.

- Any operators who decide to stay where they are will probably become bored and feel they are not contributing. This is precisely what happens in organizations when one group takes it upon themselves to separate the planning process from that of implementation.

- In the unlikely event that any of the planners decide to work with the operators in the early stage of the exercise, stop them before they leave the syndicate room, congratulate them and send them off for tea early. Otherwise, stop the exercise after 20 minutes and give everyone a tea break with no further explanation or debriefing.

- After tea, ask any observers to provide the group (or provide yourself) some impressions of what went on. Then use the notes above, plus any observations of your own, to discuss some of the issues raised by the exercise.

- The point to end on is that 'a problem shared is a problem halved (or quartered, or eighthed)'. If anyone else has a stake in the solution to a problem, involve them in as many stages of the process as possible.

- On page 42 of the participants' binders is a flowchart for clarifying who is involved in a problem and the best approach to take in order to involve them. Talk through this briefly if there is time, before moving on to the action planning session.

6. Action planning

Timing guidelines

		Minutes (approx)
4.15	Action planning	75
		——
5.30		75

Action planning

- The action planning pages serve as a pro forma for tackling the live problems which participants have brought with them.

- Depending on time, it may not be possible to work through all nine questions, and participants may need to finish their individual planning after the workshop.

- Make sure the session is structured so that everyone gets at least as far as question 6. For this question, participants should work in pairs, taking (say) 15 minutes on each of their two issues, using each other as 'outside eyes' to help them generate as many options as possible.

- Questions 1 to 5, and question 7 onwards, can be completed individually, but could also be addressed as a pair. The trainer can be flexible depending on how time is running and whether participants are willing to work beyond the official finishing time (which is, after all, a tethering factor!).

- At whatever point you choose to formally close the session, thank them profusely and bid them happy problem solving.

Further reading

de Bono, E *Lateral Thinking for Management* Penguin 1987
Goman, C K *Creative Thinking in Business* Kogan Page 1989
Pokras, S *Systematic Problem-Solving and Decision Making* Kogan Page 1990

About the author

Phil Lowe is a consultant with Harbridge Consulting Group Ltd, specializing in communication and interpersonal skills, personal effectiveness and personality assessment. A trained actor, he spent several years working in secondary and further education as a drama specialist, using theatre and creative techniques in issue-based and skills development workshops. Prior to joining Harbridge House he worked at managerial level in the publishing industry. His writing work includes the BBC Radio 4 business quiz *The Board Game*, and *Individual Excellence: Improving Personal Effectiveness at Work*, published by Kogan Page. He holds an honours degree in English from Cambridge University and a postgraduate diploma from The Drama Studio, London.

About Harbridge Consulting Group

Harbridge Consulting Group Ltd is the European subsidiary of Harbridge House Inc., founded in the US over 40 years ago by members of the faculty of the Harvard Business School. The firm is now wholly owned by its senior managers, and is actively involved in management development training and consultancy throughout America and Europe. Harbridge House's unique blend of consultancy and training is supported by extensive research facilities, strengthening the firm's commitment to the advancement of management development techniques.

Slide 1

OBJECTIVES

At the end of the day you will be able to:

- **Define accurately the nature and extent of a problem**
- **Use creativity techniques to generate potential solutions**
- **Decide on and apply the most appropriate criteria to select the best solution**
- **Apply these skills to a real-life work issue**

Slide 2

Slide 3

A PROBLEM-SOLVING MODEL

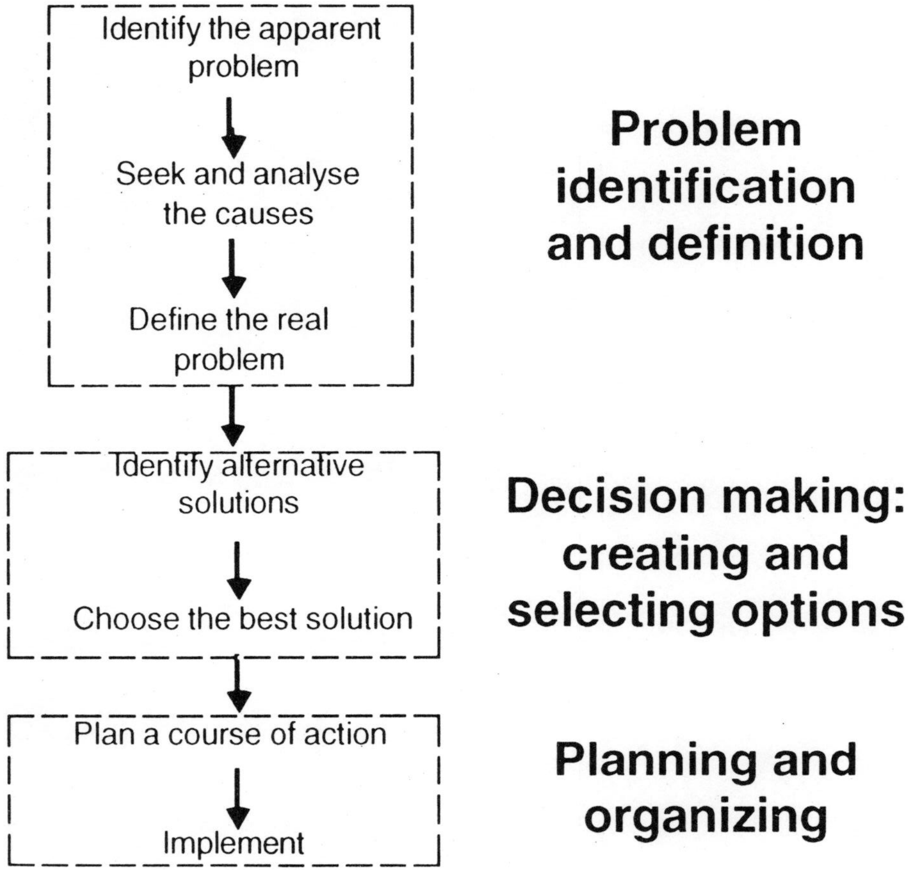

Slide 4

FISHBONE DIAGRAM

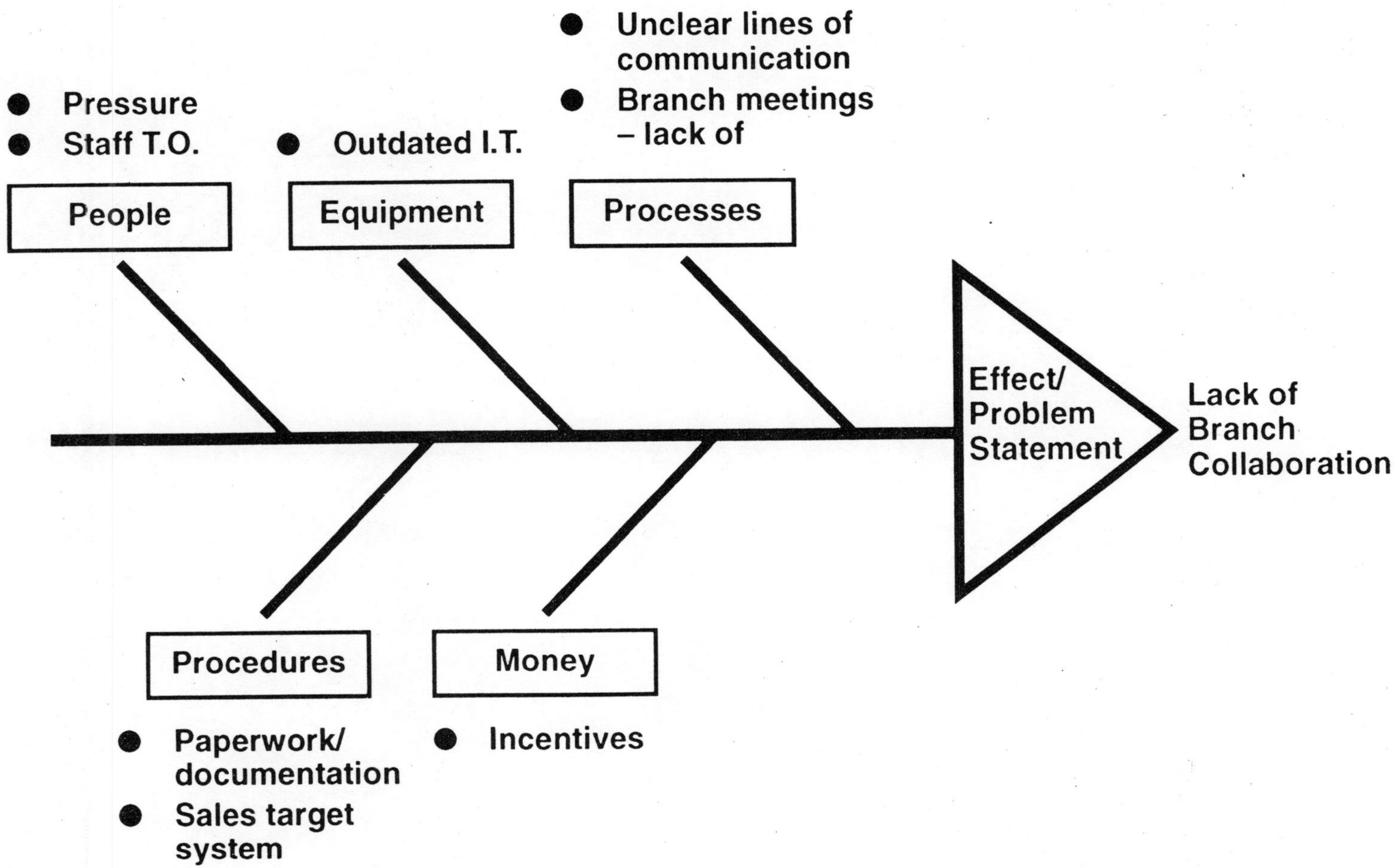

Slide 5

FORCE FIELD ANALYSIS

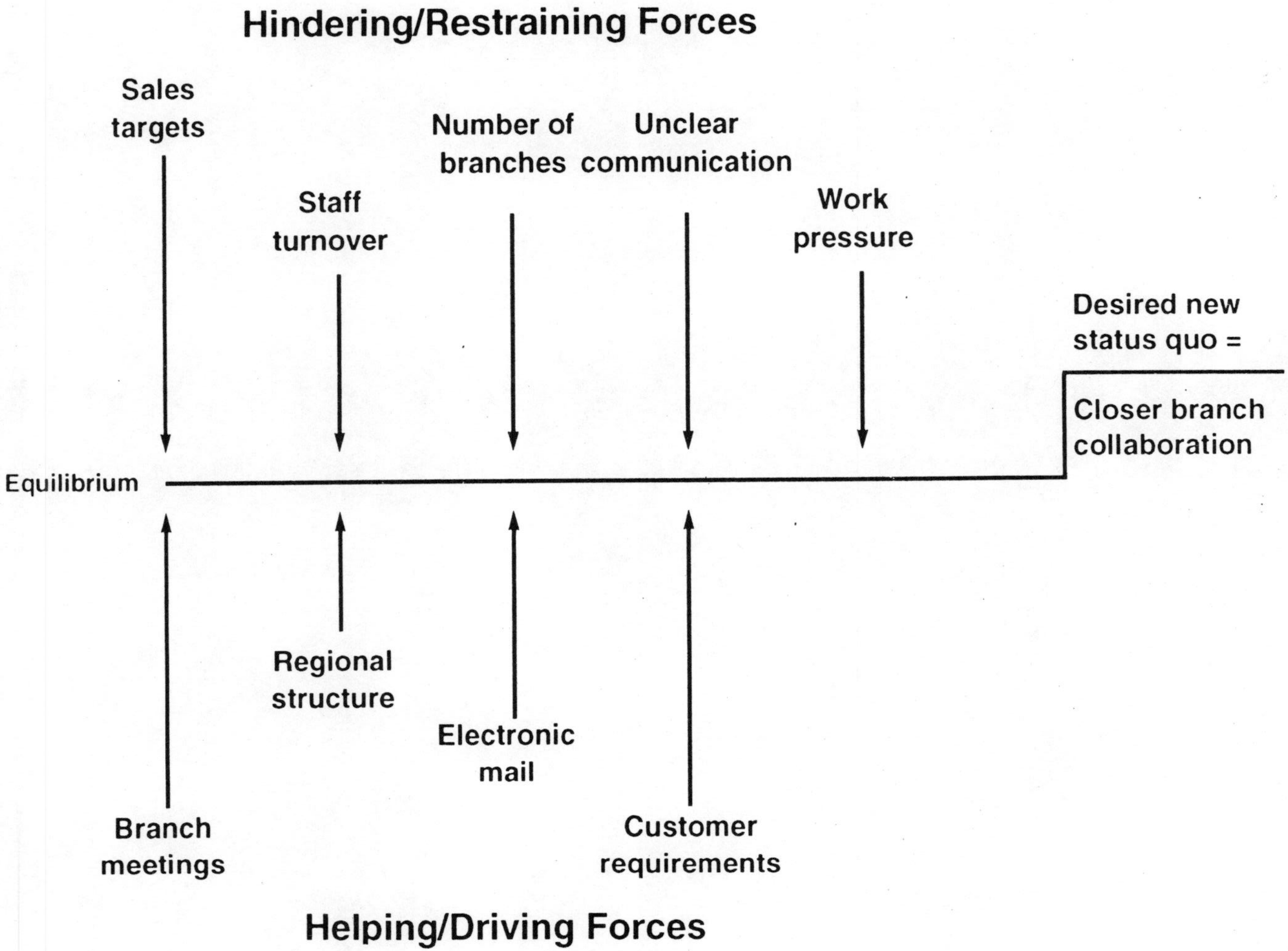

Slide 6

EXAMPLE OF AN AFFINITY DIAGRAM

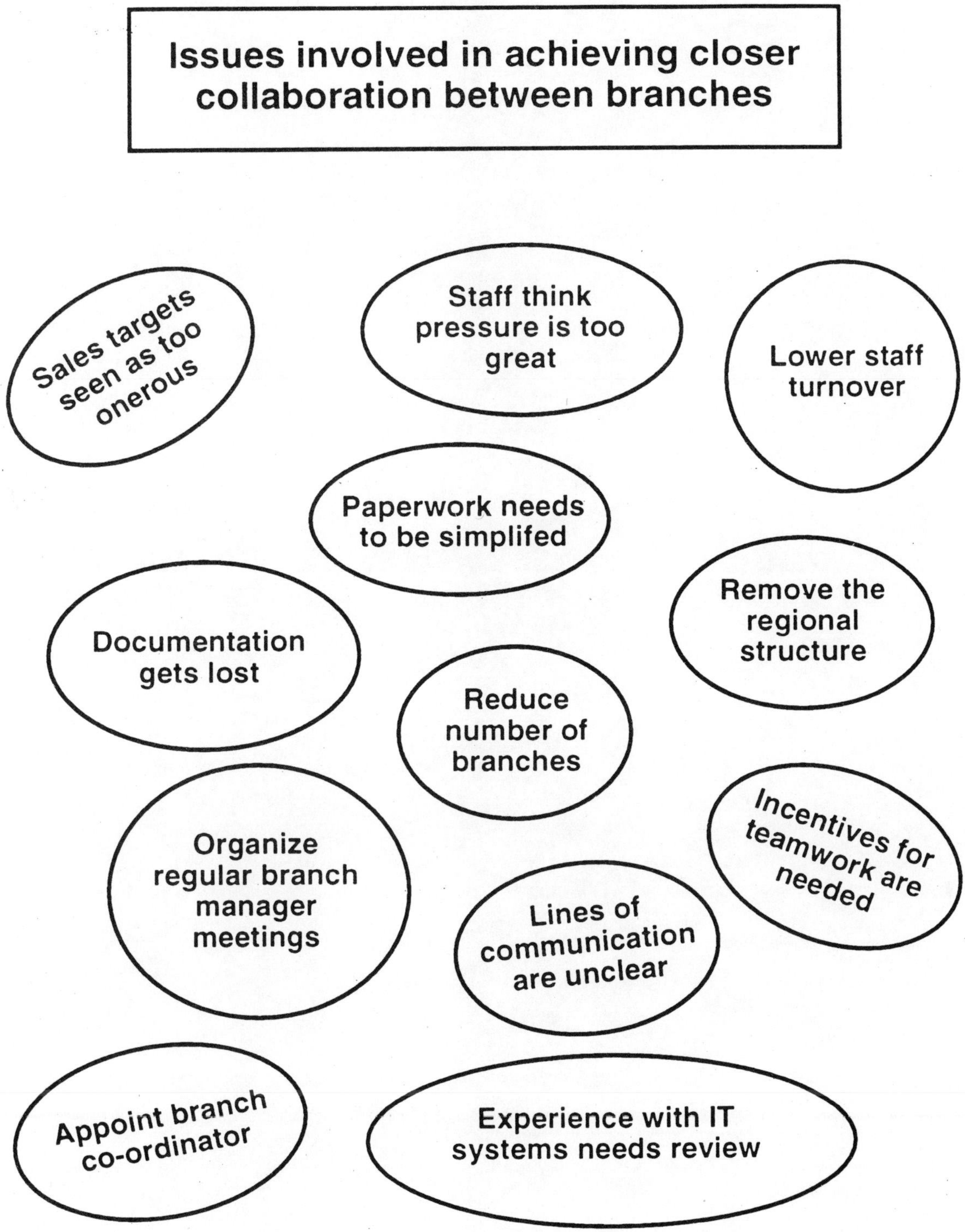

COMPLETED AFFINITY DIAGRAM

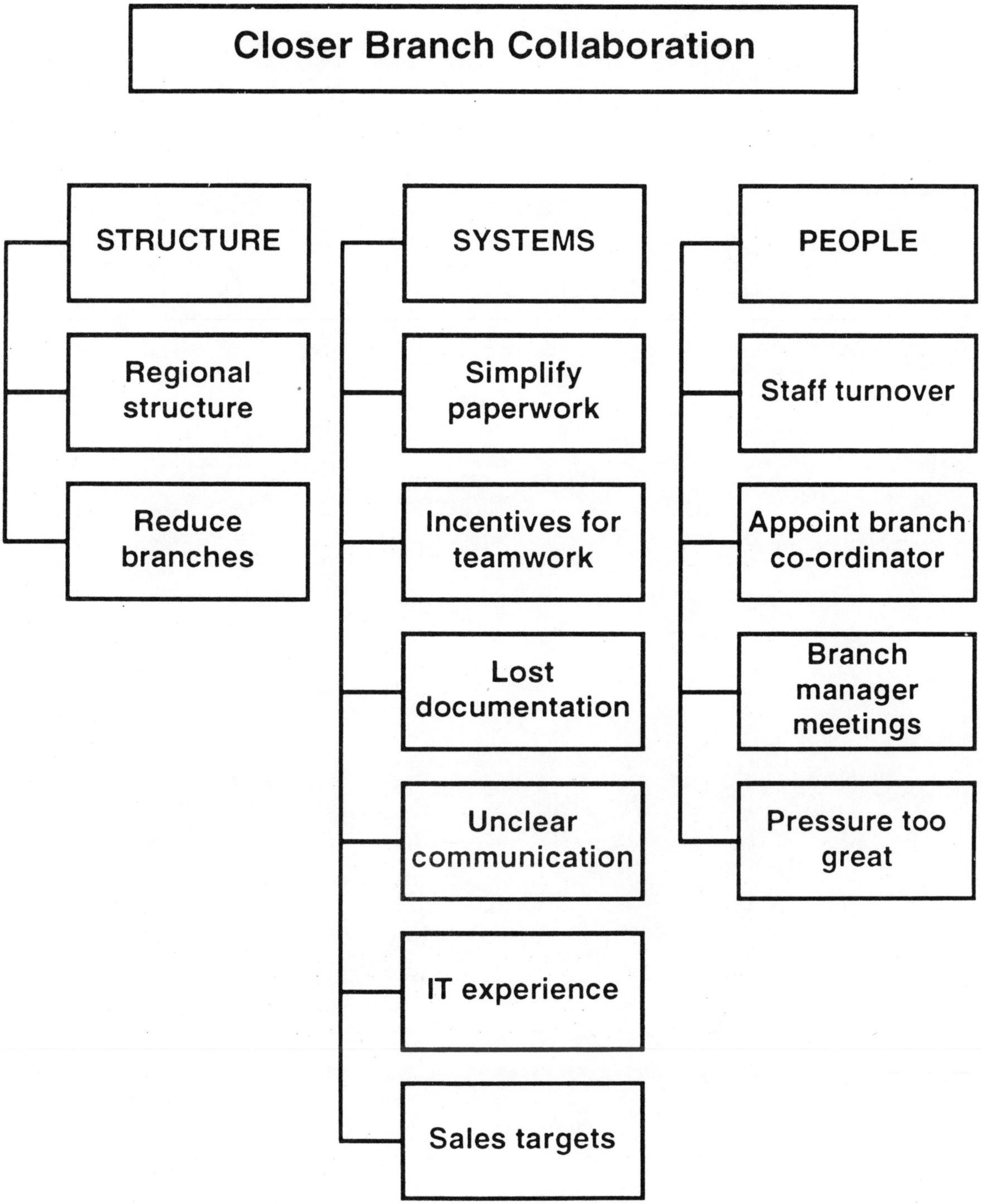

Slide 8

‘The need to be right all the time is the biggest bar there is to new ideas’

Edward de Bono

Slide 9

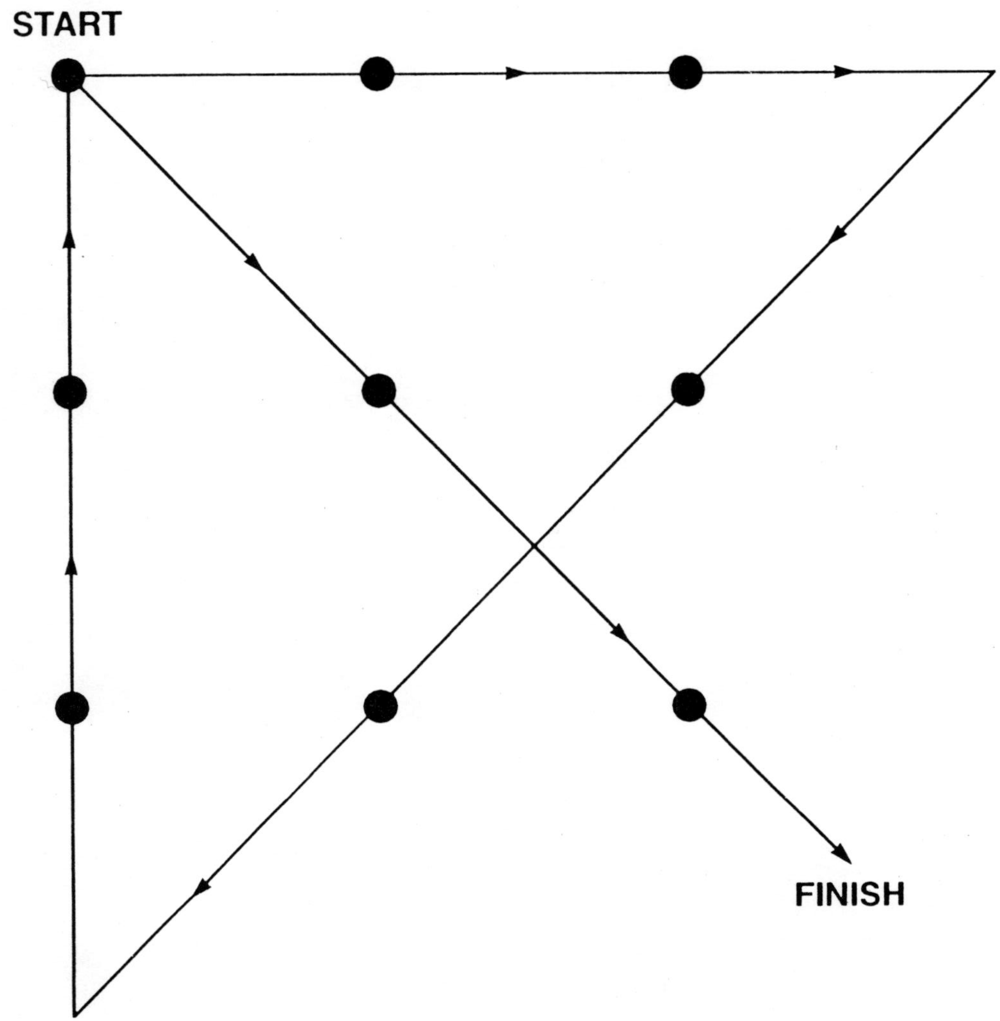

Slide 10

IDENTIFYING SOLUTIONS – BRAINSTORMING

- **Limit length of session**
- **Don't interrupt**
- **Don't evaluate**
- **Elect chairperson and scribe**
- **Have a structure**
- **Use 'tools'**
  - **Morphological analysis**
  - **Random word generating**

Slide 11

MORPHOLOGICAL ANALYSIS

Nouns

Adjectives	A	B	C	D	etc
1					
2					
3					
4					
etc					

EVALUATING IDEAS

- **Think of the context**
  - **not your own opinion**
- **Use tools**
  - **Options/criteria matrix**
  - **Risk/payoff matrix**
  - **Quality/acceptance matrix**

Slide 13

OPTIONS/CRITERIA MATRIX

How do I get from Birmingham to Edinburgh?

	Car	Coach	Rail	Aeroplane	Horse
Speed					
Cost					
Ease					
Convenience					
Timing					
Risk					

Slide 14

RISK/PAYOFF MATRIX

		Payoff H	Payoff L
Risk	H		
	L		

Slide 15

QUALITY/ACCEPTANCE MATRIX

Need for Acceptance	Need for Quality: H	Need for Quality: L
H		
L		

Handout 1

Planners' briefing sheet

Task

Within 20 minutes you are to:

- Decide how to instruct the operators to classify the total number of doors in the building
- Instruct the operators

Criteria

The doors are to be classified by:

- Material of manufacture
- Type of handle
- Finish

No instructions or communication are allowed with the operating group after 20 minutes.

Handout 2

Operators' briefing sheet

You are to carry out a task to be given to you by Planning. You may be called at any time but should report before the end of 20 minutes to the planners as no instructions may be given after this time.

Please record your feelings while you wait.

PARTICIPANT'S GUIDE

CREATIVITY

AND

PROBLEM SOLVING

Contents

Objectives

The aim of this workshop is to provide you with an understanding of, and opportunity to practise, the skills and techniques required for creative and effective problem solving.

At the end of the day you will be able to:

- Define accurately the nature and extent of a problem
- Use creativity techniques to generate potential solutions
- Decide on and apply the most appropriate criteria to select the best solution
- Apply these skills to a real-life work issue

1. Introduction

Use this space for your 'top of the head' writing

Exercise: nine dots

Your task is to join the nine dots below, using no more than four straight lines, and without lifting your pen or pencil from the paper.

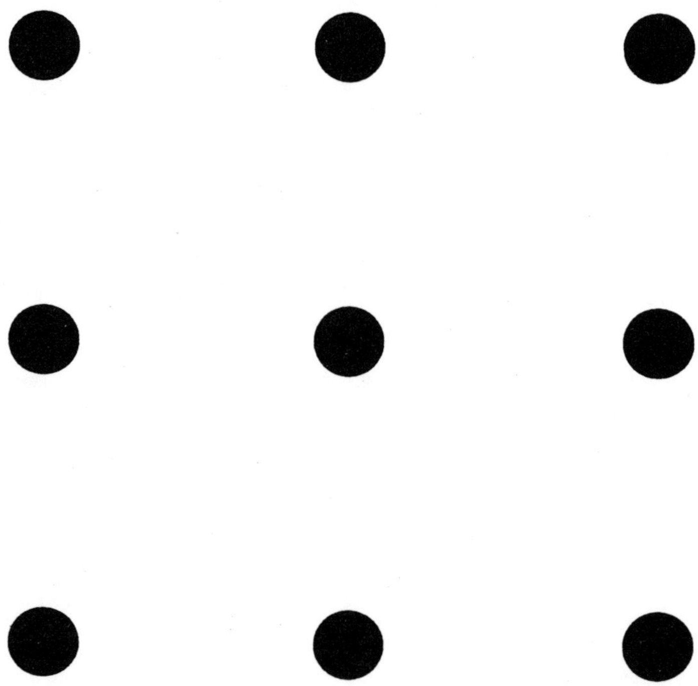

A problem-solving model

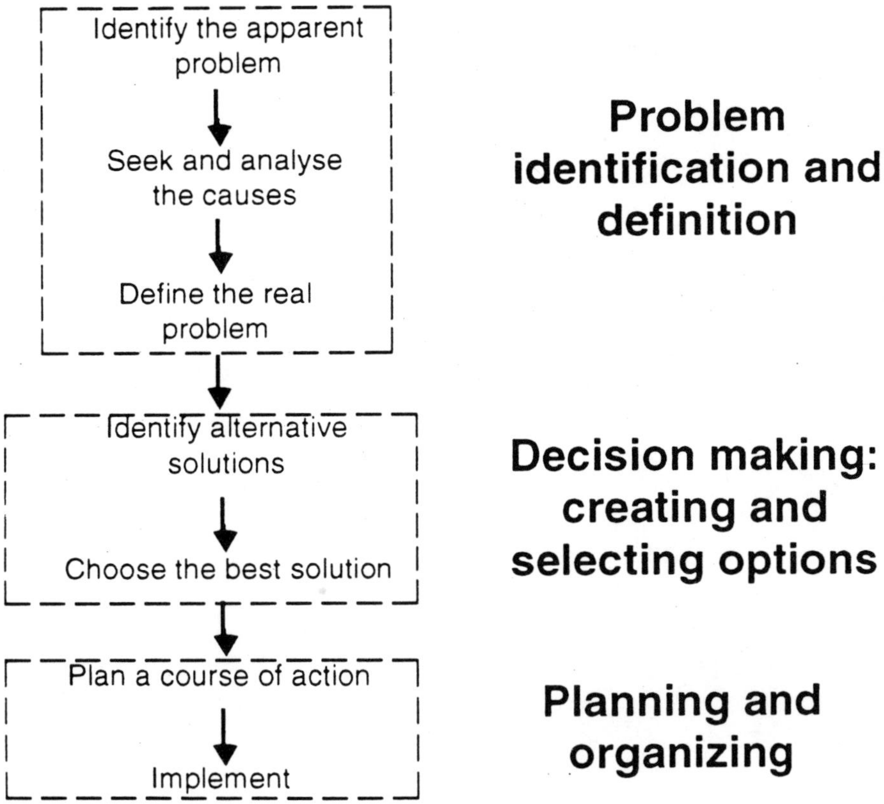

2. Problem identification and definition

Introduction

The first stage in the effective management of tasks is problem identification and definition. Before a manager can 'do' anything he or she must first consider what it is that needs to be done.

Problem identification and definition can be divided into three steps:

1) Identify the apparent problem
2) Seek and analyse the cause
3) Define the real problem

Identify the apparent problem

Very often there is no clearly defined problem to which the manager can come up with solutions. Most problems are messy, ill-defined and hard to spot with no one willing to take responsibility for them. The task of identification and definition is a key skill for any manager but one that is often seen as an impediment to the real business of solutions - taking action and doing things, instead of thinking. There are of course problems that do present themselves as clear cut - but often this means that the implications beyond the immediate situation have not been thought through. Identifying and defining problems uses two key skills: creativity and critical thinking. These two skills are used to transform a messy, ambiguous, vague problem into a more clear-cut analytical framework.

Values and context

You will note that the words 'values/context' appear in the fuzzy problem. 'Values' means all the biases, viewpoints and frames of reference that we, as individuals, bring to a particular issue. It is fairly obvious to any good manager that different individuals will tend to look upon a whole range of problems from a consistent standpoint which, for ease, can be labelled their values. Some people will have values which in management terms orient them towards the task, others towards people. It would also be surprising if the roles and functions of people did not have a large influence – sales being biased towards expansion and growth regardless of the issue, for example. In more general terms, a number of psychological tests will pick up and help individuals understand their own biases.

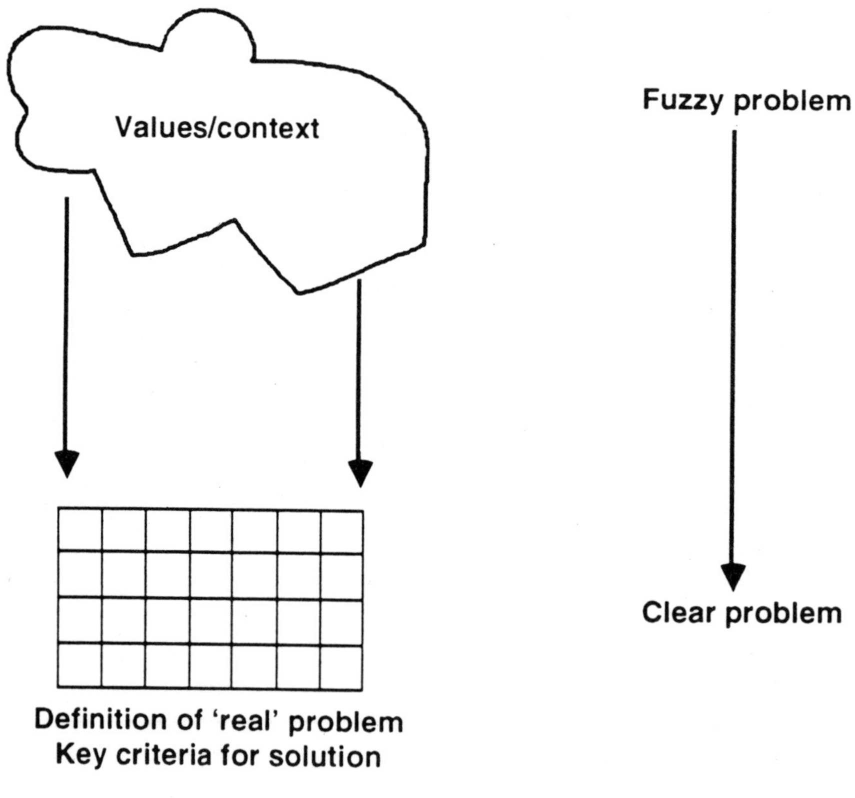

Problem Transformation

'Context' means the whole range of background variables which again influence the problem although they may only do this very indirectly. Here are all the many assumptions and company parameters. For example, a key contextual factor which most managers would take into account, even if not clarified, would be the overall company purpose and objectives. Linking into this would be the type of people in the organization, the role of the department, and the environment both internally and externally. Most problems can be seen as subsets of larger problems:

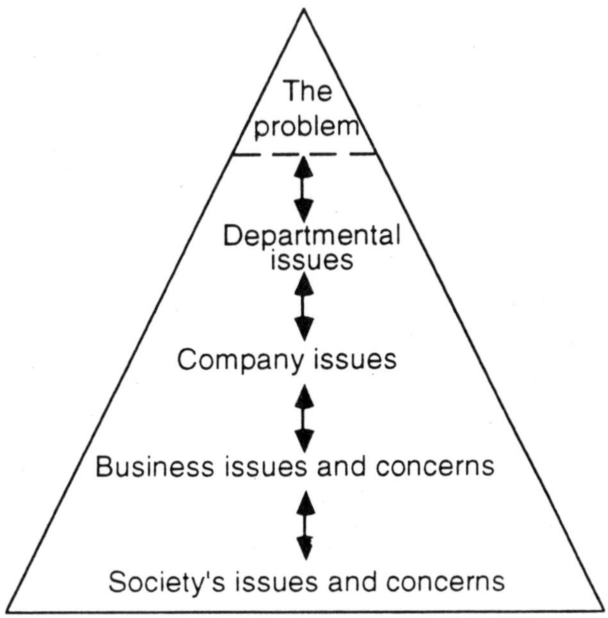

Figure 2. Problem Context

Of course, it would be extremely timewasting to re-examine all these deep contextual issues every time a decision is needed on whether to have a cup of tea or coffee, so usually the context is taken for granted in the form of assumptions. However, the more senior the managers are, the more important the context becomes. Directors, for example, need to be far more aware of the role of their company in relation to society's issues and concerns than, say, a production manager. Sometimes in problem identification there is a need to re-examine basic issues (growth, company purpose, etc.) and this possibility should be allowed for.

Seek and analyse the cause

Critical thinking is used to judge what the key decisive factors are that affect a problem and to see whether it needs to be redefined. Data and facts need to be collected, if not done so already, to help in this clarification. There are several techniques that are used at this stage to help organize data and ideas so that critical judgements can be made more easily. The techniques are used to organize data visually to help assimilation and any visual presentations such as pie charts, histograms, graphs or flow charts should be used wherever possible. Two of the key techniques are:

- Fishbone diagrams (Ishikawa)
- Forcefield analysis

Fishbone diagram (cause and effect)

After collection of factors and data, three or four key areas into which they can be placed are identified. These will vary but often key groupings used are:

- People
- Processes
- Materials
- Money

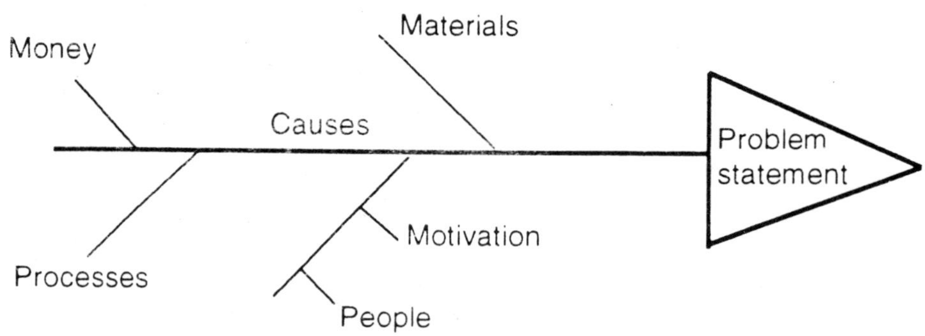

Fishbone Diagram

Force field analysis

Force field analysis, developed by Kurt Lewin, is used to describe a situation in terms of a balance between two sets of forces - helping and hindering. For example: helping forces for low morale could be pay and conditions, hindering forces could be poor supervision, etc. Situations can be represented graphically as shown below.

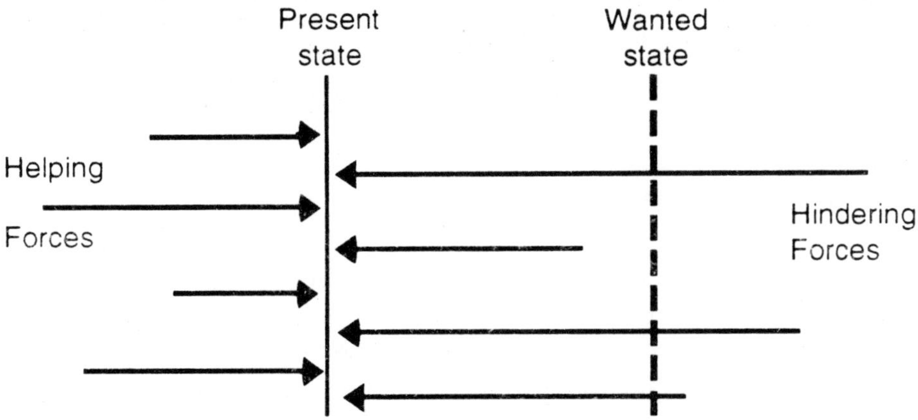

Force Field Analysis

First, the forces on both sides must be identified. Then they must be weighted in terms of the amount of force they exert. You can bring about change in two ways: by increasing the forces helping change or by reducing the forces resisting change. The most effective way is to weaken the resisting forces. The procedure is as follows:

1. Choose a particular problem that you feel is worthwhile working on.

2. Define in terms of (a) the present situation and (b) the situation you would like to see when it is solved.

3. Make a list of forces impacting on the situation. These can be people, money, time, external factors – anything that could hinder or help you to make a change. When identifying forces, it is helpful to be specific and to draw a force field diagram.

4. On a force field diagram draw the forces with the arrow signifying its strength of each (the longer, the stronger).

5. For each hindering force list the actions you could take that could possibly reduce or eliminate the force.

6. For each helping force, list the actions you could take that could possibly increase the force.

7. Determine the most promising steps you could take towards solving the problem and identify the resources available to help you.

Affinity diagram

An affinity diagram can be used to uncover the various aspects of a particular issue. It is particularly useful when issues are large and complex or when a significant breakthrough is needed. Examples might include the need to identify expectations of specific customers and customer segments, or to isolate the issues involved in implementing a new IT system. The steps involved are:

1. Generate – using brainstorming techniques – a full list of all the issues involved in the situation selected (e.g. all issues relating to closer collaboration between a company's sales branches).

2. Write each issue on a card, Post-It or even magnetic hexagon. Each issue should have a noun and a verb (e.g. 'documentation gets lost').

3. Place all cards, Post-Its, etc. on a flat surface so each member of the group can see easily.

4. Move the cards around until there is agreement about the clusters. Each cluster forms a grouping with similarity of meaning.

5. Label the clusters by giving each a 'header' note that captures the central theme in no more than five words (e.g. 'lost documentation').

6. Consolidate the result onto a flipchart or large sheet of paper so the overall problem can be seen.

Problem definition

Clear problem definitions are brief and to the point. They are specific and concrete. They say what the problem is without implying a particular solution in the definition. They are also understandable to all those involved.

Linked to the one-line problem definition should be a list of criteria which give guidelines and parameters defining acceptable ranges of solutions. These will emerge from the analysis. For example:

Problem Definition	Fall in sales in last period	
Criteria	*Must:*	Sales up to budget targets by next period
	Would be nice:	Recover lost sales from this period

Finally, the whole question of problem ownership emerges. There needs to be a clear definition of the boundaries of ownership. It is all too easy to get drawn into solving other people's problems and neglecting the ones which are your own. This is where the area of prioritizing and delegation comes in. Once the problem is identified and defined - who owns it and needs to take responsibility for it?

Exercise: Grinding Solutions plc (1)

This exercise is designed to allow you to practise problem identification and definition skills.

The task

Read the following case study, 'Grinding Solutions plc'. You are a member of the senior management team, about to attend the meeting called by the Managing Director to determine the reasons why the PT 121 Grinder-Sorter is not doing as well as it should. Details are given in the case. After reviewing it you are asked to work in your teams and produce a 5–8 minute presentation. This should include the following:

- A clear concise definition of the problem.
- A full analysis of all factors impinging on the issue. This should include visual presentation of data. A force field analysis, fishbone diagram or affinity diagram must be included. In the analysis the key relevant factors should be identified along with those considered not to be relevant.

Grinding Solutions plc

Grinding Solutions is a fairly small firm specializing in the complex technology of grinding materials of all kinds to powder and then distributing the powder in a controlled manner into various combinations of finished materials. Applications are many and varied, ranging from food manufacture to paint combination to waste disposal. The company's turnover is not large, about £10m in 1990. It employs about 95 people in all. The organizational chart is as follows:

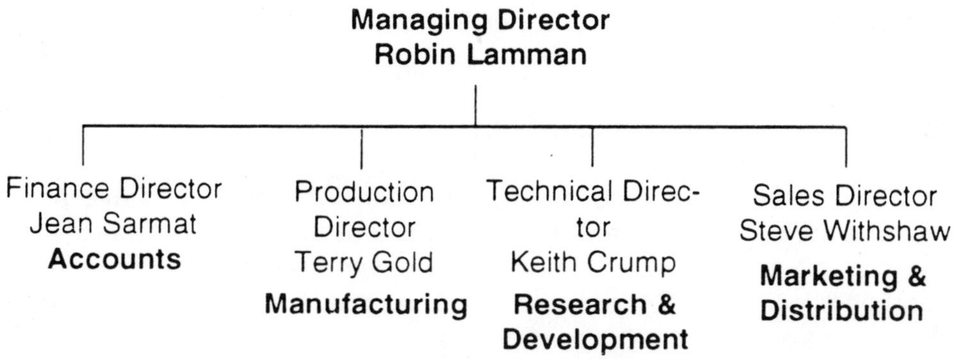

Organization Chart

There is no personnel function as such. Each director takes care of the staff working for them with the MD taking responsibility for wage negotiations. Relations between the Directors are not at their best. The Sales Director has always felt that the Managing Director has no understanding of what Sales is about. He feels frustrated at what he perceives to be the lack of vision and drive.

For example the Sales Director has been convinced that there is a considerable potential for a market to be opened up in the developing countries of Africa. The MD, however, is unconvinced and is demanding market research and figures to prove this; he is also worried about problems of foreign exchange.

The Technical Director is brilliant at introducing new concepts and is often called upon to deliver papers on some of the advances he is making at Powder Technology conferences. However, his people skills are about zero and he seems to spend his time ignoring the needs of those who work for him or doing the same to members of other departments.

The MD is good on detail but sometimes seems to get sidetracked in terms of priorities. He spent a lot of time recently looking at a possible new layout for the assembly plant which the Production Director felt somewhat annoyed about as he considered it to be his job.

The Finance Director has only been with the company for two months and is still in the adjustment phase, trying to understand the particular intricacies of this company's accounting systems.

All in all, then, a reasonably typical Board.

The previous year, Grinding Solutions launched their most versatile product aimed at the agricultural market – the PT 121 Grinder-Sorter. This has the latest micro-electronic scanners and is able to cope with grain products over a wide range of conditions – wet, dry, small sizes, large sizes. It is sold at a premium over the competitors of about £100. Sales are mainly through the 35 distributors upon which the eight sales people call.

Initial profits with the PT 121 Grinder-Sorter were as hoped, but there seems to have been a falling of sales and hence a loss in the last six months. The Managing Director has called a meeting of the senior managers and wants you all to try to determine exactly what is causing the problem and what the most useful course of action should be.

TO: Directors
FROM: Robin Lamman, Managing Director
SUBJECT: PT 121 - Sales and Profitability

I am extremely concerned by the loss of sales on the PT 121. Why is this happening? What are you doing to improve things?

I want to see you all to discuss this at a special meeting. Check with Cynthia for the time.

Figures are given below. They are not good.

Month	Number Sold	Gross Sales £	Direct Cost £	Profit/Loss £	Qrt
1	37	22200	27773	-5573	
2	64	38400	31013	7387	
3	79	47400	32813	14587	16401
4	77	46200	32573	13627	
5	60	36000	30533	5467	
6	48	28800	29093	-293	18801
7	41	24600	26587	-1987	
8	32	19200	25506	-6306	
9	17	10200	23706	-13506	-21799
10	33	19800	25626	-5826	
11	23	13800	24426	-10626	
12	21	12600	24186	-11586	-28038

Internal Memorandum

As one of the senior managers getting ready for the meeting you have been thinking about the problems associated with the PT Grinder-Sorter. As usual it is difficult to pick on any one overwhelming focus for concern. There seems to be a variety of problems, some of which you suspect have arisen because of lack of communication in the top team. Their meetings are poor, there is no attempt at keeping to the agenda and certainly no allocation of responsibilities or actions agreed upon. There are also some not-so-hidden agendas between the Directors.

For example, the Production Director, Terry Gold, is at odds with the Technical Director, Keith Crump, over the manufacturing process. In his view the technical aspects of the PT Grinder-Sorter have taken priority over efficient production. He feels that he should have had more time to design the assembly line and that some of the quality control procedures are redundant. In fact, he has been complaining that time is being wasted by his staff. He calculates that the shop floor could produce up to 175 units a month for the same fixed costs. Actual production was 90 units per month for the first eight periods that the PT Grinder-Sorter was on the market. The recent periods have seen a fall in production:

Month	Production Units
1-8	90/month
9	80
10	80
11	50
12	50

The shop floor workers are none too happy either. The Production Director is upset because he feels that the Managing Director, who is conducting current wage negotiations, is out of touch with the production department staff. The MD has insisted that there be some changes in working practices to allow for part of the increase. One of these changes, in the Production Director's view quite an inappropriate one, is the removal of the tea-trolley and the range of home-made snacks that come with it. Now the workers have to make do with vending machines and, worse, there is no universal tea break. People have tea as and when the machines become slack. There is no opportunity for people to get together in the cafeteria for 15 minutes to have a joke and relax. Besides the social aspect, they often used to exchange the odd bit of information about the practicalities of the production line which used to save repetition of mistakes. However, the Managing Director, in the Production Director's view, seems to have exchanged a common sense approach for an efficiency expert's dubious opinion. The staff now spend a lot of their time complaining about management who don't understand the practicalities of life.

The shop floor personnel are also upset at what they see as the constant changes in the production of the PT Grinder-Sorter. In the words of the shop steward: 'My members are highly skilled staff; they see the interference of the Technical

Director and the Managing Director as a vote of no confidence in them. Feelings are running high and the recent cuts in production on the PT Grinder-Sorter mean that they are concerned about their jobs. There is no way that redundancies can be allowed. I only wish that the managers knew how to manage instead of interfering with us. They are forcing us into considering industrial action'. As mentioned before, the situation is not helped by the interest that the Managing Director is showing in the factory assembly layout.

There is a problem with the sales force. Over the years sales staff turnover has been at the industry norm; now however, more sales people are leaving to join competitors. Last year six sales staff went in all. One of them in the exit interview complained that they were being expected to sell the PT Grinder-Sorter without adequate training. She remarked on the complexity of micro-electronics and the wide range of control settings needed to make the full use of its potential. 'No-one', she complained, 'has thought about clear instructions for the lay person, let alone us. Why didn't the Sales Director get us a product training course? The details alone took me days to understand. And for what? A miserable £20 incentive for selling each unit? That's just stupid'.

There have also been complaints from distributors about the lack of help they were getting from the sales force. Two distributors actually cancelled their contracts because they were so upset by the poor margin, as they saw it, on the unit. One of the distributors in East Anglia complained directly to the Managing Director that Grinding Solutions seemed not to have thought of the distributors' needs. He indicated that a rival, the more specialist FarmMix, gave a lot more than the miserable 15% offered by Grinding Solutions. He also said some customers felt that the Grinder-Sorter was over-priced at £700. FarmMix offered a fairly similar product for £100 less, even though it was definitely not as versatile. Maybe the customers didn't understand the extra benefits they would get for the additional £100, which again goes back to distributor and sales rep training.

This would fit in with the complaints about the adjustments needed to use the micro-electronic scanners to their fullest capacity. This unit seems to be breaking down very frequently, although the problem appears to be confined to a small number of customers and distributors. The trouble it causes seems to be out of all proportion to the numbers involved. It's the old 80-20 rule again. The product development department under the Technical Director insists that there is nothing wrong with the scanners and that they are not being adjusted properly when in use. One of the engineers said quite strongly that it was like giving a Jaguar to someone who didn't understand that oil was needed and then complained if the car broke down. In his opinion the customers who were complaining should be charged call-out rates to fix the Grinder-Sorter instead of offering free service under the warranty. He went on to say that the field service engineers had so much work to do that they couldn't waste their time dealing with irate customers; their job was to fix machines as quickly as possible and then move on to the next site.

Production costs are another source of concern. The purchasing department has warned that the sheet steel used in the PT Grinder-Sorter is going up by 4% next month. It is suggested that savings may be made on the bearings used. By going to a less rigorous quality specification, which might be acceptable to the technical department, about £7 per unit would be saved.

To make life even more difficult there may be a strike at the company which supplies the present bearings. The strike may be a long one and Purchasing are recommending stocking up on bearings or going to an alternative supplier. The Finance Director, however, in the short time she has been here, has already pointed out that the company carries too much inventory. In her view there is about £20,000 too much. Given the present interest rates, not to mention storage and handling costs, the company could probably save at least £3,000 a year by reducing the inventory.

The Technical Director's chief product engineer has been studying the costs associated with the PT Grinder-Sorter. He thinks that production costs could be cut by 20% if the following were done:

1. Combine the two processes used to stamp the shell and top cover into one process. Savings on waste: 15%.

2. Use cheaper alloy in the gears. Savings: 10% of costs.

The Sales Director's team want to increase advertising to promote the Grinder-Sorter even more. Direct mailing, local radio spots (a mention on Tomorrow's World?), etc. They want to increase their budget by 4% but are running into conflict with the Managing Director who is not convinced. He is insisting on more market research and positioning of the product – sorting out the distributors, getting more promotional material, etc.

Everyone has different views on what is best. The picture isn't all gloom either. One of the sales reps, Mary Brown, has sold five Grinder-Sorters this month and can't understand why other reps aren't doing as well.

3. Generating creative solutions

'The need to be right all the time is the biggest bar there is to new ideas'

Edward de Bono

Introduction

Many people think there is a mystical secret to creative thinking. Nothing could be further from the truth: creative thinking is simply the process of allowing your own brain to work for itself without the restrictions of procedures, traditions or the opinions and tastes of others. Unlocking the power of your brain can be approached in many ways.

A brain in two halves

Psychologists think of the human brain as operating in two distinct halves: the left and right brains. The left half of the brain is concerned with logic, reasoning, analysis, numeracy and language; the right with rhythm, music, colour, images and shape recognition. When we meet someone for the first time, the left side of the brain remembers their name, the right remembers their face.

Creative thinking often requires us to shut down our left brains – which we tend to use most of the time – and make more use of our right brains to think in images rather than words and systems.

Getting out of the box

Edward de Bono coined the phrase 'lateral thinking' to describe this process of breaking away from our normal approaches to problems in order to generate as many potential solutions as possible. De Bono talks about 'tethering factors': these are the restrictions on creativity which tend to strangle new ideas at birth.

For example, at a very basic level, someone given the task of ordering new furniture for the office will instinctively reach for the catalogue left by the office supplies rep last time he or she called. Why? Because that is the way office furniture has always been ordered. Getting away from this tethering factor could be something as simple as ringing every supplier in the phone book to generate as many ideas as possible; or perhaps talking to people in the office about what kind of furniture they would like in an ideal world. Why be restricted to office furniture? Why not have armchairs if that makes people more comfortable and happier in their work surroundings? (There may be plenty of good reasons why not, of course: but the assumption that there will is in itself a tethering factor, because it stops the idea from even being suggested.)

In the case of the 'nine dots' exercise, the tethering factor which prevents many people from solving the puzzle is the way that our brains perceive the dots as forming a box: we assume that we are not 'allowed' to go outside this box, but without doing so we cannot solve the problem. We tend also to assume that we have to use a normal size pen or pencil to draw the lines: why not use a paintbrush thick enough to cover all the dots with one straight line? This is what de Bono meant by lateral thinking: a sideways step away from our inherited assumptions about the 'right way' to do things in order to generate more potential options.

Brainstorming

Brainstorming sessions are the traditional forum for this kind of thinking. Many people are frightened of brainstorming sessions, either because they are worried about having to come up with a brilliant idea, or because we think of them as undisciplined and therefore difficult to control. If these worries are inhibiting creative thinking, then the solution is to impose some rules on the session: far from restricting creativity, the right kind of rules can make a session far more productive, since everyone knows what is going on and how the meeting is going to work.

Rules for brainstorming

- *Limit the length of the session.* Don't go on and on if people's ideas are drying up. Decide in advance how long you are going to spend (preferably a short, focused session: half to one hour) and if ideas are still flowing at the end, arrange another session rather than over-egging .

- *Don't interrupt.* Allow other people the space they need to get their ideas out. You may think yours is better – but you'll get your turn too!

- *Don't evaluate.* That would reinforce the idea that there is already a right and wrong solution. Evaluation can be done when all the potential solutions have been generated. If it is done too early it is being done on the basis of 'vertical' thinking (e.g. what we did last time).

- *Elect a chairperson and a scribe.* You need someone to keep the meeting on track and moving along. The chairperson ensures the rules are followed. It is also essential to have someone to capture every idea on paper, in order that each can be properly evaluated at a later time. The briefest, quickest idea may well be the best – but may well get forgotten if no proper record is kept.

- *Have a structure.* Don't let the meeting sprawl. Be clear about what the problem is that you are tackling, any parameters on its solution, and any essential items that the meeting has to tackle. Then agree an agenda accordingly.

- *Use tools.* Good ideas don't arise magically from the ether – at least not for most people. If you find it difficult to come up with creative ideas to order, there are techniques you can use to aid the lateral thinking process. Two of them are described below.

Random word generating

This is a straightforward technique for getting individuals or teams out of an ideas 'log jam', and away from tethering factors. The technique involves opening a dictionary or any book at random and choosing a word, without thinking about either the word's meaning or the problem being tackled. The word chosen must then be linked to the problem using as many meanings, nuances and connections as possible.

Example

The problem: How can we reduce the firm's costs without making staff redundant?

Word chosen at random from the dictionary: Limber.

Associations produced:

1. Limbering up → getting more supple → can we 'loosen up' links between departments so that things get done more quickly?

2. Limber → flexible → how flexible and multi-skilled are our staff? Could we reduce expenditure on temps if under-utilized people within the firm could take over other people's jobs?

3. Limber → rhymes with timber → wood → are our office desks/furniture made of wood? Might another material be cheaper? If they aren't made of wood, might wood be cheaper?

4. Other definition of limber = detachable part of gun carriage → are any parts of the firm detachable? Would they be more efficient broken off into separate units?

5. Other definition = gutter → drainage → waste → how much 'clutter' is there in our offices? Could we make more efficient use of space and move to smaller premises?

Many people find themselves resisting a process like that shown above, for a number of reasons:

- *It's trivial.* It is. Like many of these processes, it's a bit like a party game. But if it produces just one viable solution, then it's worth doing. Accusations of triviality are based on the tethering factor that problem solving has to be serious and meaningful.

- *The ideas don't have anything to do with the original word.* Nor should they. As long as they have something to do with the problem, the process has worked. This accusation is based on the tethering factor that problem solving is about following a logical process. It can be, but that comes later!

- *Most of the ideas are useless/unworkable.* Probably. But again, as long as at least one is useful, the process has worked. Without the freedom to produce any idea, the creative chain in which new ideas are sparked off by old ones won't work. This accusation is based on the tethering factor that every potential solution must be sensible and 'right'. Remember, the need to be right all the time is the biggest bar there is to new ideas.

- *The associations from the random word are extremely tenuous.* Extremely. But as long as the word has sparked something off, it has done its job. Again, the accuser here lives in a world where everything has to display a logical connection.

The key to using techniques like this is to resist asking 'Why?' The better question is: 'Why not?'

Morphological analysis

Morphological analysis takes the random word generation process a stage further, by combining nouns with random adjectives to create new possibilities for existing ideas. It works as follows:

- *Step one*: Assemble a list of four or more nouns which are relevant to the problem in hand. For example, suppose your company is in the leisure industry, looking for ways to get more people into a nightclub. You might start with four things associated with bars or nightclubs, such as:

– Beer

– Fruit machines

– Music

– Dance floor.

- *Step two:* Using random word generating, *but limiting yourself to adjectives*, generate four or more 'qualities' which things can have. Make them completely random – don't attempt to link them yet to the list of nouns. You might come up with:

– Painless

– Factual

– Cheeky

– Transplanted

- *Step three:* Build a matrix with the nouns along the top and the adjectives down the side, as in the diagram overleaf.

	Beer	**Fruit machines**	**Music**	**Dance floor**
Painless				
Factual				
Cheeky				
Transplanted				

- *Step four:* At each intersection, brainstorm the possibilities suggested by the combination of adjective and noun. Some possibilities include:

- *Cheeky fruit machines:* Install fruit machines which tell you a joke to cheer you up every time you lose.

- *Transplanted music:* Have regular theme nights featuring music from a different country.

- *Painless beer:* Offer a voucher with every fifth alcoholic drink entitling the drinker to call in the following lunchtime for a free 'hangover cure'.

- *Factual dance floor:* Don't just use it for dancing: one 'quiet' night a week have a quiz night with prizes including free entry to the club.

The same objections are possible to morphological analysis as to random word generating. An additional one in this example might be the risk involved in some of the ideas. That's fine. There's nothing wrong with a risky solution to a problem. As we shall see later, it's simply a question of evaluating the risk realistically. People often classify a solution as risky when what they really mean is that it's very different from anything they've done before. That is exactly the kind of solution to generate: if what they'd done before had been ideal we wouldn't be sitting round now solving the problem all over again!

Exercise: morphological analysis

In your group, conduct a brainstorming session based on morpholigcal analysis to generate some new ideas for your own organization to pursue. These may be products, services, or whatever you feel to be broadly appropriate.

Remember:

- Do not worry at this stage about how suitable the ideas are. This is not a test of how right you can be. Evaluation will come later.
- Concentrate on avoiding tethering factors – and challenge anyone you think is being tied down by them.
- You may use whatever methods you consider appropriate to generate the words for the matrix. The only restriction is that the nouns you start with have some relevance to the business of your organization.
- Be disciplined and structured – use a chairperson if you find it beneficial.
- Not every intersection on the matrix will lead to an idea. Concentrate on producing six new ideas.
- You have 30 minutes for this exercise. Elect a spokesperson and be prepared to present your brilliant creative ideas.

Some rules for developing potential solutions

In order to ensure that every potential solution is explored fully, there are certain points which all those involved in the process should remember.

1. Listen first, speak second. If you don't listen properly to the ideas of others, you will not be able to contribute properly to their eventual evaluation. You may also miss out on ideas of your own which others may inspire.

2. Build on others' ideas. Someone may have come up with a potentially brilliant idea, but which has vital gaps in it. By everyone contributing, rather than dismissing the idea as unsatisfactory, something workable may appear.

3. Ask clarifying questions. Make sure you know what someone else's idea is all about – and just as important, make sure they know what it's all about! Just because you can't evaluate an idea at this stage doesn't mean you can't ask precise questions about the exact nature of the idea.

4. Allow ideas to succeed or fail without your help. People find the 'no evaluation' rule difficult for all kinds of reasons, but often because they are worried that the team will spend all its time on an idea that may prove to be no good. Provided you follow these guidelines, good ideas will make themselves known – because bad ideas cannot sustain the process of building. If there is nothing to build on it will become apparent, and the chairperson can suggest that the group moves on to a different idea.

4. Choosing the best solution

Introduction

The reason for excluding evaluation from the process of generating potential solutions is that if ideas are evaluated too early in the process, there is a double risk that the idea may not have had a fair hearing, and that the evaluation is too subjective. The process of evaluating and selecting the successful solution must wait until all the potential solutions are fully developed.

In deciding which of the options to implement, reference has to be made back to the 'must' and 'desirable' objectives. The option selected has to meet all the must objectives and as many of the desirable as possible. Effective decisions in managerial terms are a function of quality (how right technically the decision has to be) and acceptance (how willing people are to go along with the option). From these considerations a list of criteria can be developed and each option evaluated against all the criteria. For example, suppose you wanted to get from Birmingham to Edinburgh: a list of options and criteria could be developed and then entered on a matrix such as that shown overleaf.

Options / Criteria	Car	Coach	Rail	Aeroplane	Horse
Speed					
Cost					
Ease					
Convenience					
Timing					
Risk					

Options/Criteria Matrix

By allocating points to each of the criteria for each of the options the most appropriate solution can be found. Part of the process involves deciding, for example, how important speed is relative to cost.

Another useful matrix is the risk/payoff matrix.

		Payoff	
		High	**Low**
Risk	**High**	Do with insurance	Leave alone!
	Low	Do immediately	Why bother?

Risk/Payoff Matrix

Other aspects to consider in decision making are the effects of the option on other people, departments, etc. The selected option may well cause problems for others which will then have to be dealt with. Splitting complex decisions down into a set of very small, simple yes/no decisions can help to reduce the expertise needed – hence the use of flow charts and decision trees.

Exercise: evaluating and selecting options

In your groups, you are to choose one idea from those you have been given which your organization can implement. To do this, work through the following steps:

1. Decide as a group six criteria which your organization (rather than you as individuals) regards as most critical when evaluating new projects or ideas.

2. Then use an options criteria matrix to rank the ideas and select the 'top three'.

3. Take the top scoring idea and place it on a risk/payoff matrix. Does it still stand as a potential recommendation? If not, take the second highest, and the third. Which one emerges as the front runner?

4. Take your 'best' idea and place it on a quality/acceptance matrix to determine how best to approach the implementation of this innovation.

5. Be prepared to present to the whole group your chosen idea and the rationale behind its selection.

Exercise: Grinding Solutions plc (2)

Return to the problem definition you generated from the Grinding Solutions case study.

In your group, use whatever methods you consider appropriate to generate potential solutions to the problem, and then to identify the most appropriate solution or solutions.

Be prepared to present a plan containing the priorities for action as your group sees them.

5. Planning for implementation

Use these pages to make notes from the discussion following the team exercise.

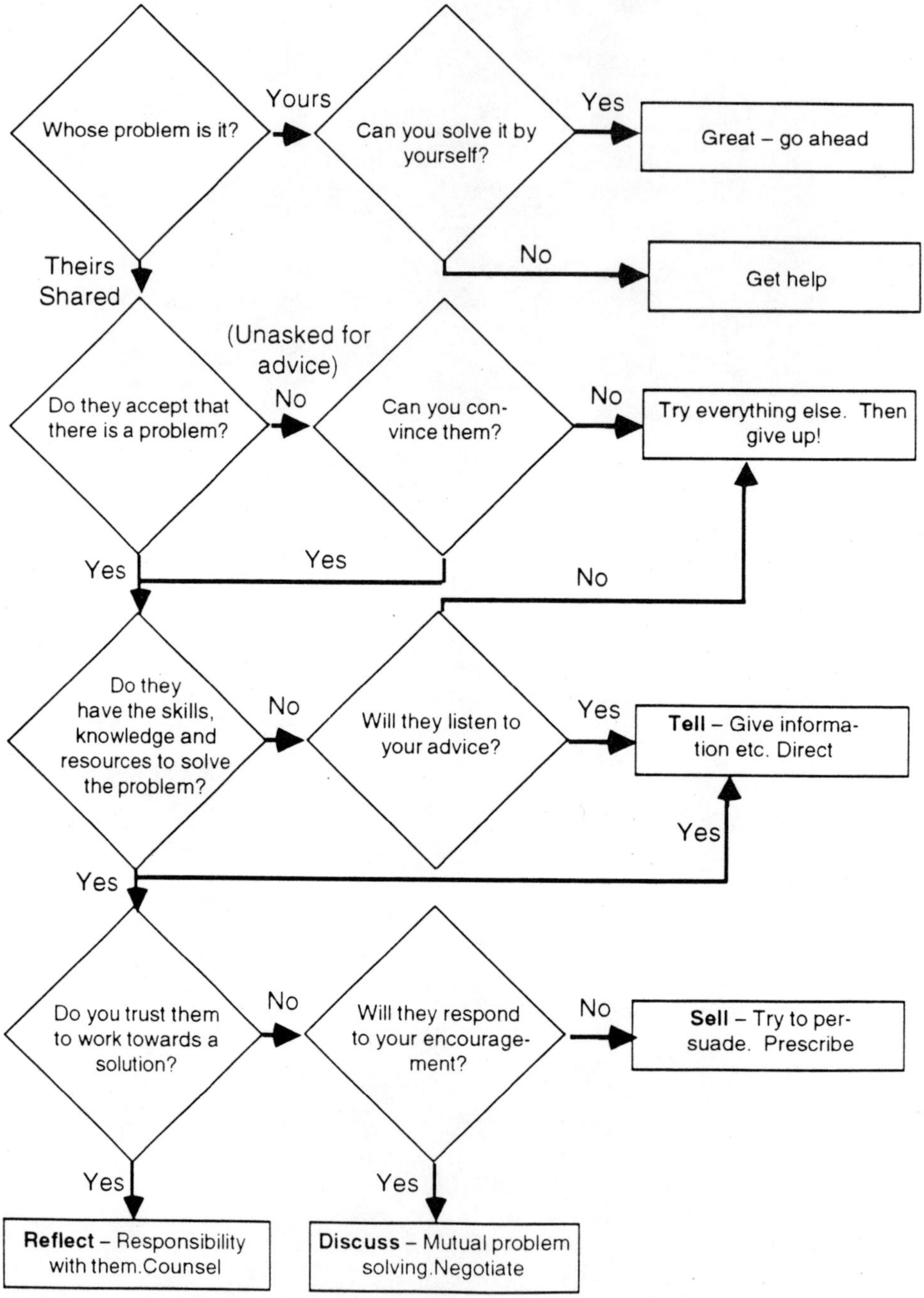

Flowchart for problem clarification

6. Action planning

This last section of the workshop is designed to give you an opportunity to tackle a live problem from your own organization.

The pages which follow ask a series of questions to be answered individually or in pairs.

You may not leave this workshop with an implementable solution: concentrate instead on using the techniques we have covered to find new and fresh potential approaches to your problem.

1. What is your concise definition of the problem?

2. What are the consequences of not addressing this problem?

3. Use a fishbone diagram or force field analysis to break the problem down into its constituent elements.

4. Now take a realistic view as to which elements of the problem are completely outside your control. List below between three and six elements which you personally could do something about (with or without help).

5. Choose one or two of the elements you have listed as being the most important: the problem as a whole cannot be solved without these being tackled first.

6. In your pair, use an appropriate and structured brainstorming method to generate as many potential solutions to your one or two 'mini problems'. Do not evaluate at this stage. Use this and the next page to summarize the options you generate.

7. Now use whichever combination you prefer of options/criteria, risk/payoff and quality/acceptance matrices to evaluate the potential solutions. Choose between one and three solutions as your front runners.

8. Consider your chosen solutions and answer the following questions:

   – Who needs to be involved?

   – Whose approval needs to be gained?

   – How long might be needed for implementation?

   – What is the likely cost?

   – Are there any implications for working practices, systems etc, in the organization as a whole?

9. Be as definite as you can about your priorities for action in the space below:

Further reading

de Bono, E *Lateral Thinking for Management* Penguin 1987
Goman, C K *Creative Thinking in Business* Kogan Page 1989
Pokras, S *Systematic Problem-Solving and Decision Making* Kogan Page 1990

About the author

Phil Lowe is a consultant with Harbridge Consulting Group Ltd, specializing in communication and interpersonal skills, personal effectiveness and personality assessment. A trained actor, he spent several years working in secondary and further education as a drama specialist, using theatre and creative techniques in issue-based and skills development workshops. Prior to joining Harbridge House he worked at managerial level in the publishing industry. His writing work includes the BBC Radio 4 business quiz *The Board Game*, and *Individual Excellence: Improving Personal Effectiveness at Work*, published by Kogan Page. He holds an honours degree in English from Cambridge University and a postgraduate diploma from The Drama Studio, London.

About Harbridge Consulting Group

Harbridge Consulting Group Ltd is the European subsidiary of Harbridge House Inc., founded in the US over 40 years ago by members of the faculty of the Harvard Business School. The firm is now wholly owned by its senior managers, and is actively involved in management development training and consultancy throughout America and Europe. Harbridge House's unique blend of consultancy and training is supported by extensive research facilities, strengthening the firm's commitment to the advancement of management development techniques.